MUSING WITH CHARLIE

A Short Story

by

Gordon Morris

ARTHUR H. STOCKWELL LTD
Torrs Park, Ilfracombe, Devon, EX34 8BA
Established 1898
www.ahstockwell.co.uk

© *Gordon Morris, 2020*
First published in Great Britain, 2020

The moral rights of the author have been asserted.

All rights reserved.
No part of this publication may be reproduced
or transmitted in any form or by any means,
electronic or mechanical, including photocopy,
recording, or any information storage and
retrieval system, without permission
in writing from the copyright holder.

British Library Cataloguing-in-Publication Data.
A catalogue record for this book is available
from the British Library.

Arthur H. Stockwell Ltd bears no responsibility
for the accuracy of information recorded in this book.

ISBN 978-0-7223-5019-5
Printed in Great Britain by
Arthur H. Stockwell Ltd
Torrs Park   Ilfracombe
Devon EX34 8BA

CHAPTER 1

THE RESCUE

The wind is enough to cut even a tough old bastard like me in two. Still, a man's got to do what a man's got to do. This January night is black as coal as I hear the enormous breakers on the shore and feel the horizontal rain lashing my face.

On with the wellies, don the waterproofs, tie the hood tight and take a deep breath.

He was a handsome bugger; I really couldn't have blamed any woman for being taken in by that ebony-black face, lying on his stomach looking at my partner with those brown eyes through the bars, sleek body and God-given good looks. No wonder she just melted for him. Two weeks later he was released. It took three of us to put him in his harness.

Three hundred quid later – castration fees, bowls, collars, leads, toys, food and goodies – I was then forced to suffer the indignity of being pulled like a locomotive out of the rescue centre to admiring looks and comments, mainly from the ladies. He pulled me straight into the car park, looking expectantly from one car to another then to me as if to say, "Come on, stupid – which one is mine?" I mentioned to my partner that he must be used to being chauffeured. Six months of springer-spaniel pup was to now rule my life.

Still, back to where I was: Hayling Island common and beach

in a gale-force wind and horizontal rain. My partner is snug in her warm living room covered with a blanket, Southern Comfort to hand, digesting that opium of the female population, *EastEnders* or some other neuron-destroying soap.

So I'm a Meldrew! Well, I'm almost sixty and I'm entitled to be so. All things considered, I've probably got the best deal.

Right, I open the tailgate and a flash of fur leaps out like a hyper leopard, charges around for a few minutes then crouches down and leaves a veritable truncheon. A disdainful look says, "Go on, then! Clean that one up, ya numpty." With that he's off into the darkness – a dog on a mission, the Bruce Willis of the canine world – off to sniff as much arse as possible in his allotted time, wreak as much havoc as possible, roll in the worst decaying fish, carrion and any other foul stinking mess he can find, and if possible give me, his dad, his mentor, his best friend, a coronary. Still, I love the little bugger to bits.

On these walks (or should I say endurance tests?) the mind does tend to wander! What's the attraction in arse? Huh! I can talk. When I was young the fashion gurus of the time ordained that all female backsides should be encased in tight miniskirts and hot pants. Criminal to testosterone-charged young lads like myself with hormones surging through the veins like white water! On more than one occasion, sitting on the top deck of the bus, hot sunshine pouring down on my groin through the window, I was vainly trying to look nonchalantly out of the window as if the abundance of rears walking the streets with tight blouses and naked thighs had no effect on me whatsoever. No effect? No effect! There was effect all right, and no way could I walk that long, long walk down the bus aisle. So I sat tight until many stops past my destination, desperately trying to concentrate on thoughts of waterfalls and cricket matches, dreading the thought of a female ticket inspector asking me why I had gone so far past my destination.

Of course the wisdom of old age tells you to take a carrier bag of groceries to hold in front of yourself. Alas, but of course by then nature has had the last laugh as that white water has now turned into a babbling brook. Yes, I'm beginning to understand him to a degree.

The other long walk was when the smoochy music ended and then through gritted teeth you told your partner to stay pressed up tight and she insisted on knowing why and then giggled uncontrollably upon realisation.

Still, back to the beach. I've bought the essentials for walking Charlie: ball slinger, shoulder bag with a minimum of three doggie bags (this little fella could crap for England), water, brush, collar, lead, treats, etc., etc. I look like something out of Ross Kemp's *Ultimate Force* preparing to go to war! No wonder the other dog walkers give me a wide berth. Dressed like this I'd be afraid of me too.

On one such night two police officers on patrol approached me thinking they were in for promotion for discovering the real ET. They saw the small flashing lights careering round the common at about a foot above the ground, following the contours of the land, darting here and there. They were amused and disappointed to learn it was only my Charlie wearing his battery-operated flashing collar, so I at least have a chance of keeping track of that bundle of nine months of inexhaustible energy. Still, some light relief on the long shift thanks to the little clown!

I battle on, plastic bags and flashlight at the ready. I think back to the 'rescue' again. It was a Sunday afternoon in October 2006 and, being a little bored, I suggested to my partner that we take some of our old blankets and towels to the local animal rescue centre as we had been meaning to for some time. Yes, she replied, but it was an unspoken agreement that we would be bringing no dog back with us as it was only eighteen months since her beloved dog died. There was no way that another dog could replace her dog – that paragon of virtue through her rose-tinted specs. I too loved that dog, but I saw him as he was – another three-to-five-bagger with convenient deafness, digester of decayed organic matter and roller in it, delinquent all his life, but as lovable a rogue as a dog could be – but that's another story. Anyway, an hour or so later we arrived at the rescue centre with the towels and blankets. No, it wouldn't do any harm to have a look at the wretched inmates. Minutes later her brain was penetrated by those piercing brown eyes in that black white-dappled head right through to the maternal area of her mind that he managed to instantly reduce to mash, and the deed was done. Mummy's boy from that moment on – although Dad's too, I have to admit. I loved that little miscreant from the moment I saw him.

Two weeks later, out in the car park as I've already described, I was being dragged about by this little pup whose closing statement on his CV read, 'This dog is completely nuts.' UNDERSTATEMENT! As soon as he knew which one was his, in he leaped. Satisfied with this roomy car, back seats down to give him much more room than even we had, the next half-hour was spent driving back to my partner's bungalow, tail wagging – well, everything wagging – and tongue licking everything in sight, obviously content with his new car and two new mugs.

CHAPTER 2

SETTLING IN

Arrival at my partner's house went without a hitch. He investigated her large pristine garden, making plans for his future lawn hole digging, shrub chewing, laundry burying and general yobbish behaviour.

I return to that endurance test we call a walk and encounter three more stalwart soap-opera avoiders. Three arse sniffings and one abortive soggy mounting of Baxter the Labrador. After the big chop, my Charlie has been very confused about his sexuality. But I have to hand it to him, he's a trier. My mind wanders back to that first Sunday we collected him and decided to walk him on the beach around the perimeter of Hayling Island Golf Club. This is our favourite walk on this unspoilt part of Hayling, with its ever changing seascapes over the Hayling bay and the Solent across to the Isle of Wight.

After a few hundred metres I said to my partner, "I think he will be OK off the lead," he was such a good dog.

Was he? As a matter of fact yes, he was surprisingly good, didn't run away and kept near us.

His first encounter was with Barney the black Labrador. He said hello as only dogs can and then moved on. Barney has always remained a friend.

Five minutes later he met Max the Rottweiler! Hell, what to do! He was off the lead and running towards his certain doom in Max's jaws. I died a hundred deaths in those few seconds.

But much to my and Max's very macho owner's surprise, Max wanted to play with my little Charlie and at times was running away from him. Did my chest puff out with pride for my little David, my Hermes the giant slayer? Ever since, my Charlie will play with or attempt to bonk anything from chihuahuas to Great Danes.

Great Danes! Yes, how the mind wanders and muses on these walks. Dogs have a habit when playing of running full pelt together, oblivious of anyone in their way, and knock you flying as any owner will vouch for. There I was in full wet-weather gear on the beach when he spotted the Great Dane. The giant, Arthur, held no fear for my little David and soon had him running around full pelt. Charlie brushed my leg, I turned and then the world turned twice, as all fifty-nine years of me shot up and cartwheeled (I swear more than once) and returned to earth on my shoulders.

Arthur's owner's face was full of deep concern (we live in a compensation society) for my welfare. Hell! Dogs will be dogs. I suggested he put Arthur forward for the English rugby team, or should it be Danish?

Yes, I muse and reminisce on our walks all the time; it's a kind of therapy for us old boys, I suppose.

About two weeks after rescuing him we took Charlie to Queen Elizabeth Country Park near Petersfield. Two hundred metres or so up the winding forest track I panicked. Three bloodthirsty-looking Staffordshire bull terriers were hurtling up the track heading for my little Charlie, totally oblivious to their owner's shrieks. No doubt, I thought, eons of evolution would instruct the primordial part of Charlie's brain to leg it very sharpish, and my Charlie is fast. Oh no! That part of Charlie's brain must be defunct; he flipped over, his back legs apart. What could I do? Disembowelment was seconds away – or so I thought. The mauling didn't materialise. To my and my fellow onlookers' astonishment, what occurred was nothing short of canine pornography. Three voracious female dog tongues attacked Charlie's undercarriage. The little bugger lay there in smug ecstasy. Fight or flight? (Evolutionary behaviour needs rewriting, Mr Darwin.) For a second I was certain he shut one eye and looked up at me as if to say, "There, dummy – watch and learn. Just watch and learn." I dine out on that story with the small embellishment that further on three lovely young ladies came walking towards me and – to cut a long story short, that's how I came to be on the sex offenders' register. Only joking!

The walk's over now. One stinking soaking-wet Charlie leaps into the car and I peel off the drenched wet-weather gear and my car is a sodden smelly mess with a very tired and content springer pup flaked out in the back. Trouble is it will be me in the doghouse for bringing him back to my partner's immaculate suburban bungalow like that, even though he will go straight into the kitchen via the side door and stay there till he's dry. But what the hell, I'm a man, aren't I? Yes, apparently that's the problem!

CHAPTER 3

SPRINGTIME

Charlie is one year old now. It's April 2007 and he's a one-dog demolition squad. We are walking the common after his Sunday-morning marathon swim. This two-hour expedition will knacker him out for a few hours if he can find some fellow nutters to run and play with. Then after a couple of hours' kip he will be raring to go again. Such are springer spaniels, I've found out.

It's surprising, but all the dog walkers I passed the time of day with all winter and discussed our respective charges with are completely unrecognisable without woolly hats, wellies, scarves and assorted wet-weather gear. Some are even quite attractive. Now, there's a plus! Women that wouldn't give me a second glance chat away with me as if I were family when I have a dog with me. Consoling if, like me, your looks are rather challenging, to use a PC expression – or what I was bought up to call an ugly old sod. Long gone the fresh-faced handsome young rake that used to grin back at me from the mirror!

Musing still about when we got Charlie, on that first sunny autumn morning we walked him on the beach. The Solent water off Hayling was beautifully calm, like a mirror reflecting the sun's rays. I looked at the sea, I looked at my little Charlie and then at my partner. She read my mind and gave me the 'look', but I was always a rebel and, casting caution to the wind and risking a bollocking, threw a stick into the water. That immature trusting little canine saw a flat expanse of terra firma and ran full pelt down to the water to do what only Jesus could. The look on that puppy's face as he sank into the briny blue was hilarious – bewilderment is not strong enough a word – and even my disapproving partner could not help but laugh. After a few seconds he, realising this wet stuff is fun, became a Mark Spitz or Jason Donahue of the dog world. No matter how big the breakers, or how cold, that little hero of mine crashes into them fearlessly and he very reluctantly returns to the shore.

I've had dogs as far back as I can remember – always been a dog man.

I normally work a six-day week plastering people's houses and extensions for a living as I've done since I was sixteen, and I'm sixty in May 2007. But Sunday mornings are reserved for Charlie's swim, mainly to divest him of the nasties he has been rolling in all week – unless I've managed to give him an evening swim. Then it's only a few days' nasties. Nasties! I've skipped over the worst, and on reaching one year old he is finally over the 100-per-cent recycling phase that went from discarded tissues on down. The vet had no answer but to suggest he went on the council payroll.

CHAPTER 4

THE JOYS OF DOG WALKING

Ninety-odd per cent of this book is true, but some of the names have been changed to incriminate the innocent.

Dogs are the most wonderful, faithful, loving, loyal and comical creatures on God's earth, and I love them in return. However, as dog owners know, and non-dog-owners reading this must realise by now, they do have their downsides.

Yes, safe in the knowledge that these polythene bags could never split (could they? COULD THEY!) I advance on the umpteenth truncheon of the week. This in turn reminds me of my good friends of long standing I'll call Matt and Sally. Like me, they're real dog people and have Chester, a Jack Russell, and Nobby, a little brindle terrier with the face of a comic angel. Now, it's a fact that in a long-standing relationship the lady usually has a pretty low opinion of her partner's prowess. When I was married it was long understood that if World War 3 broke out it would be my fault. It's an understanding that my local landlord empathises with, that when we are 'big boys' we will be allowed to choose our own parking space at the supermarket, etc., without the ladies' superior knowledge on the subject. I'm also sure that the builders of pyramids, the Great Wall of China, etc., wouldn't have been trusted to put a shelf up at home. However, if there is a bump in the night a mouse in the house or some mountain of a man cutting you up on the road you're suddenly expected to become a superhero and 'sort it out'. Yes, ladies, you know it is so. Trying to park at the supermarket, orders are barked out – "Park there!" – regardless of the fact that you are in the process of passing the one-metre-wide space. Later in the supermarket café, trying to drink the insipid dishwater that goes for coffee in these places, you try to explain to the suddenly mute, pursed-lips lady that you didn't go in that space simply because you couldn't with the best will in the world do a comic-book handbrake turn into it because you had a bared-teethed sub-Neanderthal bent over the steering wheel of his kiddie-crushing (bull-barred) T. rex of a four-wheel drive six inches from your rear bumper.

With this culture in mind, Matt related the details of a couple of Sunday-morning walks around the Bastion. This is some long defunct fortifications and moats in the north of Portsmouth to counter a Napoleonic attack from that direction. It is now a very pleasant landscaped walk.

Well, Nobby went missing and very quiet for those ominous seconds that dog owners know to fear.

"Go and find him," Matt was ordered.

Matt descended the stone steps in the 'arches' and was confronted by this angelic-looking terrier with a huge human sun-baked truncheon that some desperado had left gripped in his jaws.

"Get it off of him."

Matt's stomach retched and he grabbed a stick, Sally urging her 'hero' of a husband on.

"What could I do?" Matt asked me in the pub, and I was a helpless lump of breathless, manically laughing, imbecile by now as Matt can really relate a tale.

So what did he do? Well, he hit the truncheon that was protruding three or four inches either side of Nobby's jaws, with the result that it broke off and the melted filling oozed out.

Nobby obviously thought with his simple canine mind, 'Well, if he wants it too it must be good.'

GULP! Matt retched.

By this time the landlord was torn between turfing me out or calling me an ambulance.

Further on, Chester the Jack Russell saw a water rat and did what Jack Russells do with rats: bit it on the neck. Unfortunately the poor thing wasn't killed, but left screaming in agony by the side of the moat while Chester shook himself and strutted off very proud of himself. Once again Matt instantly became a superhero in Sally's eyes as she ordered him to do something. Now, Matt is a big man of fifty-something and to look at him, like me, you would not want to meet him in a dark alley. As with most macho-looking men, Matt and I are sheep in wolves' clothing and wince at the thought of hurting a fly. Still, we are men, and men have to be men in these circumstances. With a heavy heart Matt had to utilise his stick and put that poor creature out of its misery with many a stroke until merciful silence prevailed.

Such are the joys of dog walking. As I'm remembering these expeditions, Charlie has disappeared over the shingle bank for those dreaded seconds. I knew it – he's tucking into a decaying, stinking fish. I get him off it and into the car. Big mistake! He's standing behind me as I drive, his head on my shoulder with rotten fish on his muzzle, breathing stinking fish into my face.

Why do I love him so?

CHAPTER 5

SHEILA'S BENCH

About halfway around the perimeter of the golf-club fence, there is Sheila's bench. This was put on the common just fifty metres back from the beach in memory of the wife of one of my builders. Sheila was a gentle matriarch of four children, a retired state-registered nurse who tragically died of cancer a few years ago.

By the time we reach Sheila's bench Charlie is quite thirsty, so I chained a plastic bowl to it with a painted message from Charlie asking people to top it up with water and it's been quite a success, providing a water-hole for dogs and a resting place for humans. Sheila's family have inscribed it with 'Rest your body and refresh your spirit', and when you sit there looking over the Solent to the Isle of Wight it does do just that. I often rest here and put the world to rights with fellow 'Meldrews'. Charlie sits beside me, ears pricked, looking left and right, looking for humans bringing potential playmates and abortive rape victims for him. He will then run off within his safety zone, do the business and return to sit beside me and wait for the next victim.

I do my best musing and reminiscing on that bench. I remember when I first started walking Charlie. I approached the bench, which was occupied by two children, their parents and a Dalmatian. Why is it we dog owners expect much more of our animals than we do ourselves? The Dalmatian approached Charlie and was abortively pulled back by Mum.

"He never comes back to me when he is enjoying himself," she complained to me.

"Would you?" I replied, to the instant amusement of Rod.

"What?"

I repeated it.

"Oh!" The penny dropped and she laughed along with Rod to the puzzlement of the children. Every child knows their parents are asexual.

I remember having a break and a soft drink with my karate instructor some years ago and idly watching his German shepherd dog reaching the parts people simply cannot.

"I bet you wish you could do that," I smirked.

"Give him a biscuit and he'll probably let you," he said, grinning.

I collapsed as if hit by one of his infamous karate chops.

I sit on Sheila's bench and think back twenty years to when I was working for her husband, a 'gentleman builder' with a public-school manner.

I was separated and filing for divorce while living very comfortably in a local spa to the anger of my 'dear' wife. One is supposed to suffer in a bedsit, apparently.

Shortly after this, my plastering partner (I'll call him Jack) left his wife and I put him up and we enjoyed this life for a while. The girls seethed.

Our builder, also a keen yachtsman, kindly invited all us lads in the firm to an evening's sail around Chichester Harbour.

"Thanks," we said, "most kind."

"I'm not going straight," said Jack, always the joker.

The day came, and with the help of a half-bottle of spirits each, and the spa girls plaiting our black wigs, we dressed in pirate gear. With plastic cutlasses, a dead chicken on Jack's shoulder and a half-inflated parrot on mine we made the best panto pirates ever. Thirty years old was Jack, and I was forty.

A taxi ride later and we invaded the office of the boatyard owner (another builder mate) and attacked him, pissed out of our minds, with many a pirate term while he valiantly tried to explain to his customer on the phone what was occurring.

The lads came for us in the dinghy and we were sure our adventure would end there. No pissed pirates would come on his yacht, we believed he'd say. To our great surprise and lasting respect he welcomed us aboard. A fuzzy evening ensued. I remember hazy parts and barmaids being chatted up at Chichester Yacht Club. Jack apparently followed me to the Gents and was ejected by our mates as he was banging on the cubical door with many a pirate threat. Unfortunately I was at the bar and his drunken eyes had mistaken a woman going in the Ladies for me. I'm sure she didn't need to go again for many a day. The evening was ended by jealous husbands who objected to drunken pirates slapping their wives' backsides on their stools with their cutlasses. Although the wives enjoyed it.

Jack was certainly a 'lad'. I remember after a visit to the sauna he came back to the apartment looking like a cooked lobster.

"What on earth happened to you?"

"Well, you know what it's like when you're coming to the point when you have to come out of the sauna?"

"Yes!"

"Well, I was just getting there when this bikini-clad nineteen-year-old Venus came in. Oh! Yes! Testosterone immediately took effect. I placed my arms and hands to hide my embarrassment. The time came when I could stand the heat no more, but she stayed and I couldn't move until she went. Hence I'm a casualty victim. I collapsed."

He was scalded for days.

Shortly after that I played Cupid for Jack and 'Venus', and she turned out to be the love of his life. When it ended Jack turned to hard drugs and that's how a good family man can ruin his life.

It's quite amusing how many episodes in your life come back to you when walking the dog or sitting on a bench.

When Jack first lost Venus he came to see me and told me he'd been sitting in his car at the bridge for two days.

"What on earth did you do that for?" I asked.

"I was going to put a hose in the car, but as I only had a cupful of petrol they'd have found me in the morning on the back seat with a bad cough."

"You fool!" I said. "Why didn't you come and see me, your best mate? I'd have given you a gallon."

That made him laugh and loosen up a little – building-site humour.

I remember when he met Venus her dumped boyfriend threatened suicide and Jack sent him a bottle of pills to do it with. I could write a book about Jack and his exploits alone.

CHAPTER 6

THE CRUELTY OF MAN

"Charlie! Charlie!" I scream. "Come back, come back! Shit! Little bastard's gone conveniently deaf and he's on that beach angler's gear. He will nick and eat anything from the ragworm bait and prime sea bass to his sandwiches. One moment's lack of concentration and he's into mischief."

I reminded myself he was only a puppy still. Try telling that to the irate angler! I got him off and he ran away, I'm sure with a self-satisfied gait. I was trying to pacify the man, but the truth is I hate angling with a vengeance. I hate all cruelty to any creature – marine or land inhabitant.

My father was a drunken bully who even refused to allow my mother to turn the lights on on the stairs and in the bedroom to take my sister and myself to bed. Such was the extent of his meanness and bullying. I could write a book about that thug, but I'll leave it at that. The last evil thing he did to me was at sixteen, although I've only recently realised what a terrible thing it was to do to his son. He gassed himself, knowing I was alone with him and it would be me that found him. I tried to resuscitate him, but he died in my arms. I shed not a tear for him then and have not had one pang of remorse or pity for him since. Such was his drunken and sober abuse of my dear mother and us two kids.

The human psyche is, however, very complex and contrary. The one kind side of him (which I believe he shared with

Hitler) was compassion for dogs and cats. He always insisted they were well cared for, fed on time, exercised regularly, stroked and given treats. He couldn't be faulted on that subject. That is the only good thing I remember him instilling in me.

"Son, always look after them as they cannot look after themselves," he told me.

My mother was nothing less than a saint, and she often starved to try and feed us kids. Of course there was a limit to what she could do. Such was the 1950s for all working people in towns like my home of Portsmouth – life was tough, with strict rationing. I always remember the three-mile round trip I had to walk with her pushing a pram to collect coal from the merchants. My father was not one to waste what precious beer money he had on his family.

Still, I was a small child when I first got hooked on fishing and I was a keen sea angler until my early thirties. The cruelty I inflicted on my fellow creatures was horrific. The poor ragworm would be threatening me with ineffectual pincers as the hook was inserted through its head and into the length of its body; the pain must have been terrible and lasted a long time before blessed death. When we caught crabs we'd make them cross the blazing-hot road (there were not many cars) and survivors were rewarded by being returned to the sanctuary of the sea. Fish were gaffed or hooked and dragged through their reality to this alien and hostile world to have the hook sometimes ripped from their gullet to be left with eyes being burnt out (they have no eyelids), gasping for the oxygen they'd always, like us, taken for granted. Even as a small child I'd had reservations about this cruelty, but instinct, bloodlust and a lack of guidance propelled me on.

The God of the Old Testament is purported to have said, in whatever tongue He spoke, that He gave us humans dominion over all creatures. I cannot find the passage that gives us permission to breed, then kill, maim and torture them, as we do, in shooting for fun, factory farming, etc.

If anyone were to be the least bit cruel to my Charlie, then the primeval monster that lurks in the oldest part of the brain would take me over and all reason and fear would desert me in parental defence of 'my boy', to the extent that I firmly believe I would stand up to the most formidable old girls of Hayling Island.

I digress. My eventual 'road to Damascus' came when reading the following from a book by Jacques Cousteau, a twentieth-century diver and naturalist:

> One of the reasons of the popularity of angling is that mute creatures die in silent agony.

I just imagine dragging a screaming rabbit through the undergrowth on a hook.

> We look forward to the day when politicians realise that they will get more votes by supporting a fish sanctuary than by posing in a photograph holding the corpse of a giant dead fish that he and his buddies have caught to prove they are good old boys.

This change of attitude was later reinforced by reading the following by Pythagoras, a very BC philosopher: 'In the golden age of long ago birds in safety winged their way.... No trust betrayed, no hung fishes on the hooks.... Fearless in mid-field the hare would roam,' and other such pearls of wisdom.

So objection to cruelty to animals is no modern trend.

The mind wanders on. Charlie, not having a human brain, was blissfully living life to the fullest he could under my 'control'. I thought on as I walked the foreshore. Crabs and lobsters, whose only crime is to have evolved ugly to our eyes and not furry and cute with doleful eyes, we drop into boiling water. Why? Because we can. I sometimes imagine a truly civilised alien visiting our planet and being appalled at this cruelty and barbarism we humans inflict on our fellow creatures. Animals kill to survive, and with the exceptions of the feline species and orcas they usually kill as quickly as possible and do not enjoy the maiming and torture of other creatures for fun.

Now what the devil is he up to? He's in the bushes! Not a good sign. Yes, he is licking his lips and looking guilty. Oh no, he's covered in crap again! Why oh why do they have to do that? Back in the sea I put him again, which I expect he sees as a reward for getting covered in shit. He is a real water babe. Another half-hour to get the sod dry enough for his mother to accept him. We start our drying-out walk again.

I've been no angel. I was bought up in a culture where if you didn't smoke and drink you were not a man. Television adverts reinforced the myth. I started my smoking and drinking days when I was about eleven to twelve years old with the adults' blessing. By fifteen I was a regular drinker and smoker, living in a pub frequented by the Royal Navy. Seeing how the sailors acted on leave in the pub quashed my ambition of becoming an artificer in the navy. I went on with the drinking culture till I found my second wife, and ten years of sobriety followed until separation, which is when Jack and I ended up living the good life in the spa complex.

Therefore, having an alcoholic father, living in a sailors' pub and working in the construction industry, I've seen and experienced the damage drink and drugs can do to people. I have lost many people to drink and/or drugs, although they should not be separated as alcohol is just another drug. I lost an ex-girlfriend, of whom I was very fond, at an early age to drugs, so I'm qualified to have an opinion on the subject.

It was while living in the spa complex that my friend held his fortieth-birthday party for around fifty people. Another friend and I started proceedings by throwing him in the pool in his party clothes. A split second later I involuntarily followed. That was the start of a very riotous and drunken night, with men and women arriving and promptly being thrown in the pool in their finery. One poor chap couldn't swim and didn't surface until he was pulled up spluttering badly.

The morning after I awoke with three or four mates dossed on my floor, and I have never smelled such a smell before. Then promptly the cognac came up and I begged the Almighty to take me for the very last time. I've been a social temperate drinker ever since. However, we go on about drunken yobs, but we never stop to think about the way we, as a society, indoctrinate our children from the cradle into the drink culture. First we wet the baby's head with a piss-up. From there on, family get-togethers, barbecues, wedding receptions and other functions are celebrated in front of the children by a good portion of guests getting bladdered. Until we realise this and address it it's my opinion that we cannot decry the binge-drinking culture and resultant damage to our youngsters too much without accepting a lot of the responsibility, which is a prelude to my next chapter.

I look at my Charlie and smile at his canine innocence.

CHAPTER 7

A MORE SERIOUS MUSE

Bastards! It's a lovely Sunday morning and I've just walked a secluded part of our walk among the dunes and bushes and behold the aftermath of the night before. A beach party – yes, but obviously involving a large group of yobs. Broken glass, which really winds me up, is everywhere for my Charlie and others to split their paws on and hot ashes to burn them. The rest of the destruction can be put right. I walk him around the shore to avoid it. The sight gets me musing on life, the universe and everything. What's it all about? Can it really be the hokey-cokey? Sorry!

My mother instilled in me, from year one, a moral code – always think of others first, share my sweets, etc., and have principles from which I must not waver. Not so much did she do it with indoctrination, but by example. She was one of those women that the human race does not deserve, and she should have been kept in heaven where she belonged.

However, I often think she did me few favours in that respect as throughout life one has to encounter cheats, liars and other assorted dross who will con the un-streetwise among us.

I think of the two luxury yachts named *Crime Does Pay* and *Sorry, Son* – obviously a 'skier' (people spending the kids' inheritance, for those not conversant with the term). This seems to sum it up.

I was born in 1947, soon coinciding with the birth of the NHS and the welfare state, which has and will continue to look after me from birth to death. I remember that start began with inoculations, cod liver oil, concentrated and delicious orange juice and heavenly malt.

What a generation mine has been – born into austerity, youth in the sixties with the music of the Beatles, the Stones, the Who and many more, and free love (although I always insisted on charging a token fee)! OK, I for one went frustrated, but I had my principles. Until my thirties or so we lived under constant threat of nuclear annihilation, and came very close to it on two occasions, it's now been revealed. What was the advice in the event of a nuclear launch with a four-minute warning? Generally we were told to grab the nearest girl and go out smiling, or if no girls were available to put our head between our legs and kiss our arse goodbye.

Why the bonfire remains reminded me of all that I don't know. Perhaps it just jolted memories of youth, or just plain jealousy of today's conceited youth. I'm often accused of having strong opinions. Well, if a strong opinion is an objective one based on fact and reason, what's wrong with that? Surely an opinion based on indoctrination and wishful thinking is not really an opinion worth having?

Walking Charlie on occasions when the view is particularly spellbinding I'm humbled looking at the sun, moon and other celestial bodies and realising I'm actually standing on the surface of a very insignificant speck of dust in the universe. But what a magnificent speck of dust it is from my perspective.

Sometimes when I'm walking Charlie I'm awestruck at a certain sky and/or seascape and just marvel at this incredible planet that we take for granted. When I take a step back and really look, I realise that we are privileged to inhabit it for however much time we are allotted. Charlie lives for the sake of just being alive and enjoys this gift as much as he can within my imposed parameters. A zest for life is something he has taught me. Most of us humans seem to have lost that and work and/or scheme to acquire more and more possessions that give us only fleeting satisfaction.

As a Gemini (if one believes in astrology) I have a very serious side opposite my flippant and hopefully humorous and silly side. This manifests itself in skylarking and piss-taking, especially at the arrogant and pompous and particularly on-site with the lads, where we, as grown-up men do, whenever we get together, regress into childish silly behaviour. This ranges from intense water fights to the degenerate, ranging from 'pretend' mobile calls in public to those which I won't expand on.

I sometimes tell youngsters that I'll give them the most profound and useful advice they will ever receive from anyone in their life, and defy them to deny that I have enlightened them.

"Oh yeah! What's that then?" they will say or think in a disparaging manner.

I then simply tell them, "Never ever take advice from silly old buggers like me."

They always agree, but whether the ambiguity is lost on them I'm not sure. With that said, I'll now indulge myself in opinions formed sitting on Sheila's bench or walking Charlie on this foreshore or common.

Looking at the vista, which is heaven and earth, I see that creatures (with the exception of mankind) live in harmony with the earth, seasons, temperatures, nature, the sun, gravitational pull and countless other factors. All this I know as I've been lucky enough to live in the years when technology has given me, via the telly, the most extensive understanding of the planet, including life in the air, depths of the oceans and seas, deserts, forests, etc., etc. Even space has been conquered in my lifetime, and I feel privileged to have seen the moon landing (a night I'll always remember for other personal reasons – quite a large step for a young man), mobile phones, satellite images of the earth and many wonderful natural and scientific programmes in my sixty years. I am grateful for the extensive understanding they have given me.

In saying all of that, looking at the planet it's regrettably obvious that mankind is its curse. During my lifetime I've seen the human population of this incredible planet explode from approximately 3 billion in the sixties to 8 billion now in 2008, some fifty years later. Unchecked as it is now, it will be around 16 billion by about 2032. Global warming, starvation, pollution and all the other perils threatening our earth are primarily the results of overpopulation. No people, no pollution! In my schooldays I was warned about all this by a very perceptive and far-seeing teacher. I've witnessed the destruction of much of the lungs of the earth, the seas fished out, monkeys, tigers and many other species made homeless or extinct due to the relentless expansion of mankind with the justification of a human right to overbreed with impunity at the expense of all the other creatures that inhabit this finite home of ours. Perversely, that includes us.

The planet is also being depleted at an alarming rate of all natural resources: oil, minerals, trees and countless other things we depend on for our very survival. The effect, as we must be aware, is an increasing race to self-destruction. The rats left to breed in a cage scenario is what we are in now. The planet has got in the state it's in in the last fifty years or so, with not enough fish, land, oxygen, etc., to support the present population humanely.

With all the goodwill and good intentions in the world, turning light bulbs off, building windmills, reducing engine sizes and the like, it seems obvious to me that it's about as effective as farting in a hurricane or pissing in the sea. With the earth getting in this state in fifty years and approximately 8 billion people, what hope is there for the next twenty-five years and 16 billion souls? Not one in hell! Surely it's not rocket science to see that in order for the human race to survive we must take the bull by the horns and drastically reduce the human population to a sustainable level where we too can live in harmony with the planet like my Charlie.

To my simple mind the only humane way out of this dilemma is to follow the advice (if fifty years late) of my far-sighted teacher and impose compulsory reduction, as the sensible if draconian Chinese did years ago. I've worked out that the Chinese population will reduce from 1 billion to approximately 250 million in a lifetime (eighty years) if they adhere to their one-child-per-woman policy. On a global scale that would reduce the world population to around a greenly sustainable 3 billion in around eighty years if implemented now.

Yes! What a load of old bollocks that was. True, yes! But mankind being mankind, stupid, selfish and arrogant, will blindly race on to another world war, starvation and wholesale destruction in its race for the fast-depleting resources needed for each individual country. If some of the human race does survive this, I'm sure it will look back on it as the barbaric era I touched on earlier, when we practically destroyed the planet in the evolutionary twinkling of an eye. No, I haven't much respect for us as a species. And as for the God that is reputed to have said words to the effect of "Go forth and multiply and populate the earth", as much as I read Genesis I can't see where He mentions "*over*populate the earth". Even at the risk of upsetting the Church, I mention this fact.

Love? Yes, humans 'love'. As animals love their offspring we love ours and our family and partners, but as with animals it's a very self-centred love. How many let go of those they love if they see it in their loved ones' interest rather than their own? Usually we will cheat, lie and tread on anyone who gets in the way of us obtaining whomever we love. Would I let go of Charlie if it were in his best interest? I can only wonder.

I have a card with birds on the wing. It reads, 'If you love something let it go. If it comes back to you, it's yours; if not, it never was.' I feel it sums up love to me. I hope to live another healthy twenty years or so if only to see if my dire prediction is true or not. Whatever happens it will be interesting and I'll have at least another ten years of my Charlie then.

Mine was the first generation of Englishman not to *have* to go to war. And I have been, as I have already said, privileged to have lived with so much broad education, medical and scientific advances, music and many marvels, so when my time is up I hope to go very content in the knowledge that I'll be making my own one-man contribution to depopulation.

Meanwhile I live my life watching my Charlie, free of that which clutters up the human mind and musing away to myself. Go, Charlie, go – just run for the hell of it, son! Just run, boy, as I could years ago.

CHAPTER 8

GOODBYE, CHARLIE

What I haven't written is the fact that a few months after the 'rescue', the novelty of Charlie wore off for my partner. Water slopped on the kitchen floor when he drank, sand in his fur from the beach, little accidents, moulting, getting muddy and wet, etc., was too much for her, being very house-proud.

It wasn't long before she decided that Charlie would have to be returned to the rescue centre.

"No-o-o!" I said. I'd bonded with the dog and I couldn't see him going back. Living in a flat, it wasn't possible to keep him there, so I promised to sell my flat (this was early spring 2007) and get a house with a garden so I could have him permanently. It would be difficult working a six-day week, unlike my retired partner, but I would get another dog to keep him company.

Meanwhile I promised I would take Charlie off her hands as much as possible. If I couldn't take him to work I would pick him up on my way home and look after him on Sundays, etc. I also used to take him round the garden in the mornings to save her getting up early.

Thus he was, in my mind, *my* dog and I would soon have a home for him. My flat didn't sell till October 2007 and I moved into a rented flat while looking for a house and garden for Charlie and me. The weather being cooler from September onwards, I could take Charlie to work, off my partner's hands, more often now. I loved that dog as only dog lovers can understand, little sod that he is.

Every day my partner let it be known to me that she detested the 'mess' the dog made and the undertone was "Hurry up and get a garden." The pressure was mounting all year and I was doing my best to appease her, but I was bubbling up inside. Early December 2007 arrived and I was getting into bed. My partner decided to go off on one about the state of her shagpile hall carpet, blaming it on Charlie.

I said in exasperation, "Well, clean it, then!"

The response was words to the effect of "That will be a waste of time till the dog's gone."

A year of frustrating appeasement erupted, and I screamed I'd take him now and look after him the best I could in my flat until I got a garden. That night was spent in that adult way after a row, each clinging to our respective edge of the bed, bodily contact avoided at all costs.

In the morning I got up at about 6:30 a.m. as usual, gave Charlie his breakfast, made my partner a cup of coffee in bed and took Charlie round the garden to do his 'ablutions'. On completing this usual morning ritual, I gathered up Charlie's bed, food and things and put them in the car and went home to prepare for work, as is my routine. I left home for work with Charlie, giving him his morning exercise on the beach first. Returning home from work, I walked him on the beach again before giving him his dinner and getting bathed and changed myself.

As soon as I got home the phone rang. I picked it up.

"Bring my dog back," she snapped.

I lost it and screamed all the home truths. Basically she didn't want Charlie – gave him to me. She was just reluctantly helping to care for him until I had a garden. She slammed the phone down.

Let her stew! Up until that moment I hadn't considered I'd left her.

Three days went by without hearing from my partner;

though it wasn't very easy, I took Charlie to work and dried him before bringing him inside. Looking after Charlie and working meant about a fourteen-hour day for me – 6 a.m. to 8 p.m. Anyhow, on the third day I drove into my drive and got out of my van.

A police van drew up and a police officer said, "Gordon?" I thought someone else wanted a job done and me on the Christmas rush!

"You've stolen a dog!"

"What? I haven't stolen a dog!"

A WPC was with him, and what ensued to me in shock was like a surreal *Monty Python* sketch. Apparently the verbal agreement that Charlie was mine as she didn't want him wasn't legal. My partner wanted Charlie back. As he was registered at her address, there was nothing I could do. My protests that she'd send him back to the rescue centre were in vain. I then had to pack Charlie's belongings into the meat wagon, give Charlie a last hug and tell him to jump into the back of the police van.

That experience broke this old boy's heart as if he was being taken away to be put to sleep. He lay in the wagon looking at me as if to ask what was going on and what he had done wrong. They say the world is a bad place, but I believe it's humans that are the trouble.

It's Christmas 2007 now as I'm writing this little book, and I've had an offer on a house with a garden accepted. I'm looking forward to doing it up and giving a couple of new Charlies a good home. My ex-partner has offered me visiting rights to Charlie on Sundays as she's said she's keeping him now. However, I believe that would be cruel to both Charlie and me. As soon as my ex-partner gets involved with someone else that will have to end. It's a fact that like one's health we often don't appreciate what we've got until we lose it. I'd intended to write this book, if only for myself, over the period of Charlie's life, but life's not like that, is it! If nothing else this book will be a cautionary tale for anyone thinking of taking on a little bugger like my Charlie.

With hindsight I realise that the threat of returning Charlie to the rescue centre was just said in anger and frustration in looking after Charlie, who was by then more than a handful for her. What should have been a minor dispute in a good relationship with a very good woman was blown out of all proportion by stubbornness on both our sides – a lesson I've realised and taken on board.

CHAPTER 9

KID AT CHRISTMAS

I thought that was the end of this story, but it's 31 March 2008 and I've been four long lonely months missing my Charlie. Life's been very empty, and I've been living in a small flat waiting to purchase my new home with a garage and garden.

I've been given a moving-in date of 7 April 2008 and I have been looking forward to it, harbouring a forlorn hope that Charlie's mum would let me have him then, but in my heart I've been sure there is no chance.

Eureka! I've stayed home today to be able to conclude the financial details on my new home. A letter has arrived and Charlie's mum has written saying he is too much for her and I can have him back. The euphoria is incredible and I can hardly breathe with happiness at the thought of getting that reprobate back, despite all the wet and cold walks that that means.

Does that make me a masochist? I don't know and I don't care – all I want is the little bugger back home with me, his dad. I've told his mum she can take him out while I'm at work and he will have a kennel in the garage and full access to the patio area while I'm at work. This means getting up an hour earlier for him every morning for a good run on the beach or in the fields before work, but hell, he's worth it! I just remember that police van and the emptiness without him.

I've said I'll pick him up on Saturday the 5th as I'm working all week and the weather has got too hot to keep him in the van while I'm at work. A kid at Christmas! Yes, that's just how I feel, waiting for Saturday to come. I'll go to the rescue centre tomorrow and start a quest to find a companion for him and myself, so hopefully we will all have at least ten years together, I and my two reprobate dogs, and we will be happy, I hope. Ten years minimum! Yes, I hope so. I intend to get a couple of budgies to fly around the living room as well. That will complete my little family.

Marriages? I've had two and a number of relationships and a few live-ins, and for me it's as compatible as kippers and custard. I must be a miserable old bastard. However, with one or two exceptions I have remained on good terms with them.

Thinking back on the first marriage, when I was twenty-one years old, the main good thing I remember of those ten months (yes, ten) was the mouse. A mouse hole appeared in the kitchen and I was immediately Clint Eastwood. I put the cheese in front of the mouse hole, and then lay on the floor, my loaded air pistol gripped in both hands, pointing menacingly at the mouse hole. My wife too had her blood thirst up as she lay on my back. Only seconds did we have to wait before the cutest big-eared, wide-eyed little mouse face appeared. How could I? How could anybody? I dropped the gun and we both broke down laughing. There was just no way, and I'm sure that mouse lived a long and happy life and we had actually laughed together.

I wonder what that gorgeous eighteen-year-old wife of mine is like now, forty years on? I'll stick with the memory!

The second wife? Well, to be fair we had some good times before it ended after ten years. I remember one highlight when I was bored one evening and stole upstairs, stripped naked and put on a pair of her tights. Yes, the most glamorous of female attire ever, eh, lads? She was knitting on the sofa (how I hate someone knitting). I opened the door and showed a leg, and a very sexy leg movement if it had been female. A confused noise uttered from her, whereupon I bounded into the room doing my paso doble and other clumsy ballet moves and dances, well bunched up and dressed in her tights only. I thought I might be charged with murder as she took an eternally long time to be able to breathe properly. The laughing was rather unnerving as, although I'd seen them bared before, this was the first time I'd seen the fangs fully exposed down to the gums. Not a sight for the faint-hearted. That was the first and last of my ballet-dancing days, but one good memory of that prison term they call marriage.

Strange how one memory triggers another! Self-criticism is not my forté. However, looking back at the first marriage perhaps I was a little less than perfect.

Walking home with my cousin after a drunken night out, I snatched a crocus from a window box as I passed and stuffed it in my pocket for a peace offering when I got home. A little further on a taxi drew up and a sombre female voice from the back seat said, "Get in." Yes, it was my little English rose. I complied. She was on her way home from visiting her friend. Quiet ensued, and then she said in a tone only wives can use, "What's that in your pocket?"

"Oh, about six inches!" was my immediate humorously laddish reply.

The temperature dropped to absolute zero at that moment, and retribution for embarrassing her in front of the taxi driver was apocalyptic when we arrived home.

I digress. 'Tis the morrow and I'm excited about Charlie's return in a few days. It's 1 April 2008 and I've just returned home from the pet shop with my Laurel and Hardy complete with a nice large cage – two beautiful one-year-old budgies. On 7 April 2008 we will move into the new house – the home for 'the unwanted'. Laurel and Hardy I have had my eye on for months now, and if I hadn't bought them I don't think they would have sold as the babies are due in this month. Charlie is not wanted by his mum as he is too much for her, and to top it all I've been to see the most gorgeous four-month-old springer that's not wanted. I've got everything crossed that I'm going to get him, and I'll call him Jake.

On Saturday 5 April I collected Charlie. At first he looked at me in a very puzzled way as he had not seen me for four months. Seconds passed and then he went ballistic and I felt ecstatic to have him back. We got straight into the car as soon as I thought he'd calmed a little and I drove down to the seaside and common. He didn't quieten down at all, running full pelt and chasing dogs and being chased and played with. I know that watching him I was reliving my childhood when supple limbs and joints prevailed.

Early the next morning Charlie's whimpering was telling me something. Yes, I slung some clothes on and got him outside just in time. What a good lad! We all get upset stomachs, but he can't get to the loo without human help and he asked for it in the only way he could. I gave him his breakfast and uncovered Laurel and Hardy and put them in the conservatory so they could see and hear the wild birds.

Suddenly the black clouds unloaded. Snow! Snow in April? Not in many people's lifetimes here in the south of England. It hadn't snowed in years, let alone in April! Hell, it was absolutely cascading down and in half an hour we had three or four inches – incredible. Generations of kids have not seen so much snow in their lifetimes! I decided to see what Charlie thought of it. The road was empty and virgin white. He took to it like a child, running, skidding and rolling all along the road. I laughed and laughed at his antics as I haven't laughed for a very long time. I sure do love that nutcase of a springer.

After a hot bath we went down to the beach and common, covered with miles of more virgin snow – springer heaven, it seems – and he went into 'after burn', rolling and rolling in the snow. He ran up to a man.

"He's asking for a snowball," I shouted.

He grinned and lost fifty years in an instant as he scooped up some snow and threw it for my insane dog.

Not content with the cold snow, Charlie went in for a swim. I was worried – I didn't want him getting ill from the wet and cold, but he's as tough as old boots and did not seem to be at all fazed as he then rolled in the snow like a Nordic after a sauna.

Should I make an appointment with a dog shrink? No, he's great entertainment as he is and he's my therapy.

CHAPTER 10

THE DOCKIES

Walking Charlie, I glance over the water to Portsmouth – my hated home town that I left at twenty-two years old and never want to return to. My mind wanders back to childhood. Adolf's bomb sites littered the town – playgrounds to us kids; graves to the poor souls caught in them. My father was a 'dockie', an expert on torpedoes, apparently.

The dockies were welcomed to work by ear-piercing sirens heard all over town; lunch and knocking-off time were the same. Lunch and knocking-off time meant many thousands of bicycle-riding dockies, tens across and thousands deep. They rode to their respective homes across town like herds of wildebeests. Tiger tanks could not have stopped that terrifying swarm.

I've stood atop the Arc de Triomphe looking down on that incredible roundabout without rules, traffic sorting itself out, but it's got nothing on those dockies. This was the generation of men that worked through the Blitz, being a prime target of the Luftwaffe, tirelessly keeping the ships of the Royal Navy seaworthy and supplying the food, fuel and ammunition that those young seamen relied on while risking their well-being and their very lives. It was no movie.

These were the men in the 1950s and '60s that were my mentors. The way these men pedalled home for their one-hour lunch break and 'blowie' or 'noonie' for the lucky few to boast and embellish for their mates, was mind-blowing. Pardon the pun. The virgin apprentices (yes, this was before the contraceptive pill so virginity was rampant) would listen intently, fantasising about future glorious sex that hopefully would end years of sexual frustration.

I often muse on the countless young men that lost their lives or manhood before knowing the bliss of making love with the woman they love in a warm, comfortable bed. I think on this, remembering an English soldier from World War 2 fighting the Japanese in the jungle, being interviewed, saying it was OK for 'them' as they imported good-time girls for their troops. All we got was bloody Vera Lynn (a singer)! As a boy I remember working with these men. They never recounted the killing and the carnage, only the lighter moments. I remember working with a former Desert Rat who went through it all. He had cold eyes – eyes that had obviously seen terrible things. He was a small man, but had an aura of being a man that had killed and would again if need be, but he was a kind, good man that I respected a great deal.

Another veteran of the desert and Monte Cassino was a real joker and swore that as a tanker driver he had parked his vehicle on the edge of a parking area at a depot for a mundane reason, not knowing it was on fire, and calmly walked away to be greeted by fire engines. He was given a medal despite his protestations that he didn't know it was on fire. Another tale he liked to tell was his first experience of oral sex by a foreign girl and never repeated, judging by the excitement every time he related it.

His tallest story was when he and his mates were about to shoot a donkey for dinner. The padre shouted at them to stop, then dropped to his knees, took the donkey's 'donker' in hand and after a few shakes said, "There you go, lads – more meat!"

True? He swore it was, and they say fact is stranger than fiction.

Then there was my uncle after whom I was named. My mother in a light moment told me it was so because she got the wrong brother, and me having his name gave her some consolation. My uncle went through the whole war fighting in every theatre, being sunk three times. The Japanese war was worst, being attacked by the suicide planes. My cousin has photos of some of the damage: one went down the funnel of his carrier; another made a metre-wide hole in the four-inch armour of the deck. Nevertheless, despite constantly shaking, suffering from PTSD, as we call it now ('nerves', as it was known back then), he was always laughing with wickedly humorous shining blue eyes.

There was also the account I'd heard about a mother in the war who received the dreaded telegram, that her merchant navy seaman son had been torpedoed in the Atlantic on convoy duty and was considered missing, presumed dead.

Time passed and the war ended.

One day she heard the front door open and a cheery voice called, "Hello Mum." The euphoria with hugs and kisses can only be imagined.

He then explained that he had been rescued by the Americans and served the war out with them!

Not a letter! I'm sure a good hiding ensued – such are our children.

Then there was the big man that I met at a memorial service who told me he was a Royal Marine commando in the war who volunteered for the most dangerous ops because the Nazis had the affront to drop bombs on his street, killing his mother and sister. The hate and the venom he had for the Nazis was obviously still burning him up fifty-two years after the end of the war.

There were also the women that suffered and supported their men. I've heard many stories of their bravery too, driving ambulances and searching for survivors and body parts in rubble.

One stern matron on D-Day instructed her nurses to wear make-up and wait by the numerous empty beds for the coming casualties.

"Make-up, Matron?" They were incredulous.

"Yes, make-up, as your faces will be the last many of them see!"

Bravery comes in many forms.

I muse on, looking at Charlie enjoying himself doing his doggy thing and thank those poor lads for their terrible sacrifices in order that my fellow Europeans and I could live in comparative freedom and peace for these last sixty-odd years. As I mentioned before, I count myself honoured that such men and women mentored me in my formative years, by which I mean into maturity.

CHAPTER 11

MAGNOLIA COTTAGE

This is the best time of day: evening, a hard day's plastering behind me. Charlie's wreaked his havoc on the island for the day and I'm relaxing with a cup of tea. He's lying in his bed, angelic face looking at me as if butter wouldn't melt in his mouth. This is where I realise just how much I love him.

Dogs don't lie, cheat, go off in a huff, nag, have a headache or do any of the things that wind us lads up. They are incapable of polluting and ruining the planet. No matter how repulsive one may appear to other humans, dogs don't care; they just give unconditional love, especially when you come home, unlike humans. If yours does you're in the wrong house.

I haven't had a chance to look at my new home although I've had it three days now! I've a day off tomorrow, so I'll sort it then.

I've returned to writing this now in July 2008 after three months of moving and reducing Magnolia Cottage to a building site, which my 'little devil' revels in. Rubble, tools, clothes and materials – nothing is sacred to Charlie. Everything is there to chew, run off with and generally run riot with – especially with the lads that are helping me. The house is complete to the bottom of the stairs now, the garden and drive are complete, and the ground floor is still a building site.

The previous owner left a child's playhouse in the garden

and I've turned it into a kennel – Charlie's summer residence – with a very comfortable cushion and all his toys. Charlie's got a life of Riley all summer. I get up early at 6 a.m., and at 7a.m. Charlie is running on the beach with his mate and one of his girlfriends (an elderly Staffie), and finishes off with a swim. We are home by 7.30 a.m., then I'm off to work while he sleeps it off.

True to her promise, Charlie's mum comes round while I'm at work and takes him for a good run, then it's back for a kip until I get home at around 4 p.m. to give him his dinner, and later he has an hour or so's run on the common. A dog's life!

The spare bedroom is completed and carpeted and I've covered everything with dust sheets. I've rigged a three-foot swinging perch in front of one of the windows and Stan and Ollie have an indoor aviary and freedom. I love to hear their song and chirping.

Life is good at Magnolia Cottage and I'm walking Charlie. Yes, of course, miss! My mates never believe me when I tell them of the number of attractive women that stop and ask me if they can stroke my Charlie. But it's true. It's a shame, but with the good weather comes what I'll politely term the 'unsociables' – human waste, barbecue mess, broken glass and all the other rubbish they litter our beautiful sand dunes and common with, which they do in abundance.

This means I've started walking Charlie around the more isolated parts, one being the pitch-and-putt course, which does not have a Charlie-proof fence, like the eighteen-hole courses. Balls? No, he won't chase a ball unless it's someone else's. If a golfer plays a shot and Charlie spots it, sure enough he is on it and running off with it. Much embarrassed waffling later, the golfer luckily sees the funny side of my hooligan's behaviour. Nevertheless at the nineteenth hole I'm sure the golfer will protest that ball was on course for a hole in one.

Unfortunately one golfer didn't have a sense of humour and I have his No. 4 iron above my mantelpiece as my surgeon insisted on my taking it home as a souvenir, after he had cleaned it up.

Charlie is also a barbecue nicker. He can sniff one out miles away. A second's lack of concentration and sausages, burgers and chicken wings are gone. I can pretend this tail-wagging dog catching up with me is "Nothing to do with me, guv!" Charlie also loves to help me with digging the garden. Unfortunately it's usually after I've just planted the flowers.

That brings me to the garden centres. What a surreal dimension you enter there. If ever a man wants to know where females gather en masse, it's Marks & Spencer's and garden centres. Ladies with blue rinses are like a tribe of Amazons (fierce female warriors from Greek legend) at such places and leave me quite bewildered at some of their behaviour. January-sales syndrome rules, with trolleys looking like mobile jungles slamming into your ankles and bushes in your face. Still, it's planted now and I'm relaxing in my garden on a lovely evening. The budgies in their cage are dangling from the magnolia tree that my cottage must be named after, Charlie stretched out on the lawn and me with a nice cup of tea. I call him over and give him a stroke and tell him how much I love him. Crazy? Perhaps.

I look at him. Everyone says he is very intelligent. Well, what's intelligence? Different things to different people, I suppose. Is it a dog that follows his owner around at heel, sitting and retrieving at his command? Or is it my Charlie, conveniently deaf when it suits him, pushing me and his luck to the very limit? Knowing, as he does, innumerable two-word commands as long as the second word is 'off'? I'm not sure what constitutes canine intelligence, but I veer to the latter.

Well, that's about it, I suppose. I'm hopeful for around ten more years for Charlie, Ollie, Stan and me here at Magnolia Cottage. I wonder why I wrote all this, but for some reason it was prompted by my oversexed, bisexual, sex-crazed eunuch of a manic wonderful dog that I love very much!

Some months later I acquired another springer, from the rescue centre. He was called Mikey. He's eighteen months old with only one eye and a splint in his hind leg due to being run over. I had Mikey for well over two years, but due to well-intentioned but misguided people throwing stones for him, I had to have him put to sleep due to twice getting stones stuck in his gut and going septic.

EPILOGUE

I had to have Charlie put down on 7 June 2018, due to a brain tumour. I hope he and Mickey are wreaking their havoc in dog heaven.